Who
Needs
Books?

Who
Needs
Books?

LYNN COADY

Reading in the Digital Age

✖CLC
CANADIAN LITERATURE CENTRE
CENTRE DE LITTÉRATURE CANADIENNE

The University of Alberta Press

CLC Kreisel Lecture Series

Published by

The University of Alberta Press
Ring House 2
Edmonton, Alberta, Canada T6G 2E1
www.uap.ualberta.ca

and

Canadian Literature Centre /
Centre de littérature canadienne
3–5 Humanities Centre
University of Alberta
Edmonton, Alberta, Canada T6G 2E5
www.abclc.ca

Copyright © 2016 Lynn Coady
Introduction © 2016 Paul Kennedy

LIBRARY AND ARCHIVES CANADA
CATALOGUING IN PUBLICATION

Coady, Lynn, 1970–, author
    Who needs books? : reading in the
digital age / Lynn Coady.

(CLC Kreisel lecture series)
Co-published by Canadian Literature Centre /
Centre de littérature canadienne
Includes bibliographical references.
Issued in print and electronic formats.
ISBN 978-1-77212-124-7 (paperback).—
ISBN 978-1-77212-120-9 (EPUB).—
ISBN 978-1-77212-142-1 (kindle).—
ISBN 978-1-77212-143-8 (PDF)

    1. Books and reading—Technological
innovations—Social aspects. 2. Electronic
books—Social aspects. I. Title. II. Series:
Henry Kreisel lecture series

Z1003.C72 2016   070.5'73   C2015-908776-7
                              C2015-908777-5

First edition, first printing, 2016.
Printed and bound in Canada by Houghton
Boston Printers, Saskatoon, Saskatchewan.
Copyediting and proofreading by
Peter Midgley.

The University of Alberta Press is committed
to protecting our natural environment.
As part of our efforts, this book is printed
on Enviro Paper: it contains 100% post-
consumer recycled fibres and is acid- and
chlorine-free.

The Canadian Literature Centre
acknowledges the support of the Alberta
Foundation for the Arts for the CLC Kreisel
Lecture delivered by Lynn Coady in April
2015 at the University of Alberta.

The University of Alberta Press gratefully
acknowledges the support received for its
publishing program from the Government
of Canada, the Canada Council for the Arts,
and the Government of Alberta through the
Alberta Media Fund.

FOREWORD

The CLC Kreisel Lecture Series

In this event we come together, listen with more than our
ears, remove blinders and become part of the celebration,
expand our thinking and feeling of inclusion, and build
relationships.

—CHRISTINE SOKAYMOH FREDERICK[1]

THE FUNDAMENTAL OBJECTIVE of the CLC Kreisel
Lecture Series could not have been better summarized. This
series realizes most fully the Canadian Literature Centre's
mission: to bring together authors, readers, students,
researchers and teachers in an open, inclusive and critical
forum. Kreisel lecturers already include Joseph Boyden,
Wayne Johnston, Dany Laferrière, Eden Robinson, Annabel
Lyon, Lawrence Hill, Esi Edugyan, Tomson Highway, and
here the formidable Lynn Coady. Take the fine points about
social oppression, cultural identities and sense of place
by Boyden, or Johnston's reflection on the tumultuous
encounter of history and fiction. Consider with Laferrière
both the pains of exile and the joys of migrancy, or the
personal and communal ethics of Aboriginal storytelling
that Robinson presents. Antiquity and the present come
together through Lyon's lecture about the creative process
of historical fiction. Hill invokes the need for an informed
conversation about book censorship. Highway makes a
compelling argument for the liberating joy of knowing
other and others' languages, including the language of music.
In these pages, Lynn Coady's 2015 lecture urges us to assay

cultural alarmism about the future of the book in the digital age, and to reflect on what exactly we are afraid of losing, or better yet, of seeing change. Through her nonetheless very grown up and clever *Sesame Street* analogy, Coady reminds us that our latest monstrous bogeyman, supposedly lowbrow internet culture, is in reality us. She reminds us of our own agency to resist projections of fearful cultural apocalypses that the West has constructed for itself since Gutenberg's printing press ushered in modernity. Coady reminds us of our love, both intellectual and sensual, of books.

The CLC Kreisel Lecture Series confronts questions that concern us all in the specificity of our contemporary experience, whatever our differences. In the spirit of free and honest dialogue, they do so with thoughtfulness and depth as well as humour and elegance, all of which characterize, in one way or another, the nine incredibly talented writers featured so far.

These public lectures set out to honour Professor Henry Kreisel's legacy in an annual public forum. Author, University Professor and Officer of the Order of Canada, Henry Kreisel was born in Vienna into a Jewish family in 1922. He left his homeland for England in 1938 and was interned, in Canada, for eighteen months during the Second World War. After studying at the University of Toronto, he began teaching in 1947 at the University of Alberta, and served as Chair of English from 1961 until 1970. He served as Vice-President (Academic) from 1970 to 1975, and was named University Professor in 1975, the highest scholarly award bestowed on its faculty members by the University of Alberta. Professor Kreisel was an inspiring and beloved teacher who taught generations of students to love literature and was one of the first people to bring the experience of

the immigrant to modern Canadian literature. He died in
Edmonton in 1991. His works include two novels, *The Rich
Man* (1948) and *The Betrayal* (1964), and a collection of short
stories, *The Almost Meeting* (1981). His internment diary,
alongside critical essays on his writing, appears in *Another
Country: Writings By and About Henry Kreisel* (1985).

The generosity of Professor Kreisel's teaching at the
University of Alberta profoundly inspires the CLC in its public
outreach, research pursuits, and continued commitment to
the ever-growing richness and diversity of Canada's writings.
The Centre embraces Henry Kreisel's no less than pioneering
focus on the knowledge of one's own literatures. The CLC
seeks and fosters a better understanding of a complicated
and difficult world, which literature can reimagine and
perhaps even transform.

The Canadian Literature Centre was established in 2006,
thanks to the leadership gift of the noted Edmontonian
bibliophile, Dr. Eric Schloss.

MARIE CARRIÈRE

Director, Canadian Literature Centre
Edmonton, December 2015

NOTE

1. Christine Sokaymoh Frederick, introduction to *A Tale of Monstrous
    Extravagance: Imagining Multilingualism*, by Tomson Highway
    (Edmonton: University of Alberta Press and Canadian Literature
    Centre, 2015), xiii.

LIMINAIRE

La collection des Conférences Kreisel du CLC

> À l'occasion de cet événement nous nous réunissons,
> nous écoutons avec plus que nos oreilles, nous retirons
> nos œillères et nous nous intégrons à la fête, nous
> enrichissons notre pensée et notre sentiment d'inclusion,
> et nous créons des relations.
>
> —CHRISTINE SOKAYMOH FREDERICK[1]

ON NE SAURAIT pas mieux synthétiser les objectifs essentiels de la collection des Conférences Kreisel du CLC. Cette collection réalise tout au mieux la mission du Centre de littérature canadienne: celle de réunir auteurs, lecteurs, étudiants, chercheurs et professeurs dans un forum ouvert, inclusif et critique. Parmi les conférenciers Kreisel l'on peut déjà compter Joseph Boyden, Wayne Johnston, Dany Laferrière, Eden Robinson, Annabel Lyon, Lawrence Hill, Esi Edugyan, Tomson Highway, et désormais la formidable Lynn Coady. Pensons aux fines observations de Boyden sur l'oppression sociale, les identités culturelles et le lieu; ou à la réflexion de Johnston sur la rencontre tumultueuse de l'histoire et la fiction. Tenons compte avec Laferrière des épreuves de l'exil et des joies de la migrance; ou de l'éthique personnelle et communautaire du récit autochtone que nous présente Robinson. L'antiquité et le présent se réunissent dans la conférence de Lyon au sujet du mode créatif de la fiction historique. Hill plaide le besoin d'une conversation informée sur la censure des livres. Highway défend l'apprentissage libérateur et heureux *d'autres langues, de la langue des autres*, y compris le langage de la musique. Dans ces pages, la conférence 2015 de Lynn Coady nous incite à analyser l'alarmisme culturel quant à l'avenir du livre à l'ère numérique, de réfléchir à ce que nous craignons de perdre, ou encore, de voir changer. À travers de son analogie *Sesame Street* pourtant bien mûre et astucieuse, Coady nous rappelle que notre tout dernier épouvantail monstrueux, la culture internet supposément peu intellectuelle, est, au fait, nous-même. L'auteure nous rappelle notre propre capacité de résister aux projections d'affreuses apocalypses culturelles imaginées par l'Occident depuis l'imprimerie de Gutenberg et son inauguration de la modernité. Coady nous rappelle notre amour tant intellectuel que sensuel des livres.

Les Conférences Kreisel du CLC abordent les grandes questions qui nous concernent tous et toutes dans la spécificité de notre vécu contemporain, peu importent nos différences. Dans une intention de dialogue libre et honnête, ces conférences reflètent l'ardeur et la profondeur intellectuelles ainsi que l'humour et l'élégance des neuf auteurs extrêmement doués et présentés jusqu'ici.

Ces conférences publiques se consacrent annuellement à perpétuer la mémoire du Professeur Henry Kreisel. Auteur, professeur universitaire et Officier de l'Ordre du Canada, Henry Kreisel est né à Vienne d'une famille juive en 1922. En 1938, il a quitté son pays natal pour l'Angleterre et a été interné pendant dix-huit mois, au Canada, lors de la Deuxième Guerre mondiale. Après ses études à l'Université de Toronto, il devint professeur à l'Université de l'Alberta en 1947, et à partir de 1961 jusqu'à 1970, il a dirigé le département d'anglais. De 1970 à 1975, il a été vice-recteur (universitaire), et a été nommé professeur hors rang en 1975, la plus haute distinction scientifique décernée par l'Université de l'Alberta à un membre de son professorat. Professeur adoré, il a transmis l'amour de la littérature à plusieurs générations d'étudiants, et il a été parmi les premiers écrivains modernes du Canada à aborder l'expérience immigrante. Il est décédé à Edmonton en 1991. Son œuvre comprend les romans, *The Rich Man* (1948) et *The Betrayal* (1964), et un recueil de nouvelles intitulé *The Almost Meeting* (1981). Son journal d'internement, accompagné d'articles critiques sur ses écrits, paraît dans *Another Country: Writings By and About Henry Kreisel* (1985).

La générosité du Professeur Kreisel est une source d'inspiration profonde quant au travail public et scientifique du CLC de sonder la grande diversité et la qualité remarquable des écrits du Canada. Le Centre adhère à l'importance qu'accordait de façon inaugurale Henry Kreisel à la connaissance des littératures de son propre pays. Le CLC recherche et entretient une meilleure compréhension d'un monde compliqué et difficile que peut réimaginer et peut-être même transformer la littérature.

Le Centre de littérature canadienne a été créé en 2006 grâce au don directeur du bibliophile illustre edmontonien, le docteur Eric Schloss.

MARIE CARRIÈRE
Directrice, Centre de littérature canadienne
Edmonton, décembre 2015

NOTE

1. Christine Sokaymoh Frederick, introduction à *A Tale of Monstrous Extravagance: Imagining Multilingualism*, par Tomson Highway (Edmonton: University of Alberta Press et Centre de littérature canadienne, 2015), xiii.

INTRODUCTION

FULL DISCLOSURE, right up front.

I had never read a single word that Lynn Coady ever wrote before it was my pleasure to spend a week in her company, on a Cuban beach, just outside Havana.

I'd heard a lot about Lynn Coady, because she'd won the Giller Prize back in 2013 for a short story collection called *Hellgoing*—after being short-listed for the same prize, only the previous year, for an astonishing novel called *The Antagonist*.

The Giller is just the latest in her growing list of literary accolades that stretches from coast to coast: Canadian Authors Association Air Canada Award for Canada's most promising writer under 30; the Dartmouth Book Award for Fiction; the Atlantic Bookseller's Choice Award; the Canadian Authors Association's Jubilee Award for Short Stories; the Stephen Leacock Award for Humour; the Victor Martyn Lynch-Staunton Award for an artist in mid-career; the Writers' Guild of Alberta's Georges Bugnet Award for Fiction in 2007 and again in 2012; and of course, the Giller.

It is not just her awards that encompass all regions of the country. Lynn Coady has lived and worked her way across Canada: she was born in Port Hawkesbury, Nova Scotia, grew up on Cape Breton Island, went to university in Ottawa, started working on her first novel, *Strange Heaven*, in Fredericton before moving to Vancouver to finish it. Eventually, she found herself in Edmonton before heading off to Toronto.

Clearly, Lynn Coady travels well. Her reputation reaches beyond our Canadian shores—I got to know Lynn Coady at the Playa del Este, on a white and sandy beach, with all of

her books, and a bottle of dark, seven-year-old Cuban rum by
our sides.

I actually *met* Lynn Coady, herself, in person, the night
before the Kreisel Lecture, over dinner, in Edmonton. Lynn
Coady is a complicated and compelling person. She's very
funny too—in person, and on paper.

Over dinner, we talked about many things. Lynn
described a golf course that's recently been built near where
she grew up on Cape Breton Island. The bizarre reality of
Asian billionaires being flown by helicopter onto a beautiful
new links land golf course, on property that was once
ranked among the poorest places in Canada, provided a clear
indication that "truth" is often stranger than fiction, which
is one of the things that gives writers like Lynn Coady the
opportunity to spread their literary wings.

We spent some time talking about unreliable narrators.
Then we talked about the new Apple iWatch. Lynn can't
wait to get one. I refuse to touch one with a ten-foot pole. We
have differing positions on technology. The question that
haunts her amidst this onslaught of technology is whether
we will still need books. I don't want to put words into her
mouth, but I think she may be arguing that we will soon
all be able to read *À la recherche du temps perdu* simply by
glancing at our wristwatches.

We've established that Lynn Coady has lived from coast to
coast, and that she gathers awards as she has moved around
the country, but her writing encompasses Canada in similar
ways. Throughout her fiction runs a common thread of wry
humour through which she explores the absurdities and
hypocrisies of life in Canada.

The first of her stories that I read (which is actually the
first story from *Hellgoing*) is called "Wireless." It's about
being in St. John's, Newfoundland—and both alcoholic

Introduction | xv

writer Jean Rhys and visionary inventor Guglielmo Marconi
play major supporting roles. You should know that I try to
spend as much of every summer as possible in St. John's, and
you probably already know that IDEAS is a radio show, and
Marconi had a little something to do with radio.

The next story that I read was called "Body Condom." It's
set on the west coast of Vancouver Island. For my sins, I've
spent some time there too. Lynn Coady absolutely nailed the
psychic geography of both those places. One of the central
images of "Wireless" is a photograph of Marconi, blissfully
surrounded by wires: "Visionaries and drinkers: obsessed
with away; looking for else."[1] In some ways that just sums up
a metaphorical truth about St. John's.

Moving on to the other coast, now, which is the setting
for the second story: I've been in bars on Vancouver's
Downtown Eastside, where Tom Waits wannabes sing songs
about accidentally killing hookers during heroine binges
in blood-splattered hotel rooms,[2] and I've visited people
in Tofino who actually spent twenty minutes introducing
me to their plants, just like the protagonist's mother does
in that story. The protagonist in "Body Condom" is first
introduced to us as "a walking erection." Lynn Coady's sense
of humour is down to earth, but it takes us right inside the
head of her character. In so much of her work, the physical
characteristics of her characters reveal their inner struggles
and conflicts.

Lynn Coady obviously understands Canada, inside
out, from sea to shining sea. She's also amazingly adept at
mastering the ups and downs of gender geography. The
protagonist I've just mentioned—whose name is Hart—is a
screwed-up but loveable guy, a person we've all met a million
times, yet Lynn Coady breathes a life into Hart that is unique.

She's good at guys!

But what woman in her right mind would ever dare to write a novel like *The Antagonist*? In it, an ultra male, hockey-playing hulk named Gordon Rankin spends thirty chapters critiquing the work of yet another offstage male, whose name is, intriguingly, not much more than Adam. Adam and Gordon are quintessential hockey-loving Canadian males. Lynn Coady could be writing about me and my friends.

Lynn Coady somehow gets inside guys' heads, and it's scary—from a guy's perspective—when a woman manages to do that. But what is significant, is that she does so with a sense of humour that is compelling. Lynn Coady's critique of the masculine world in which she finds herself is terrifyingly funny. The personal hell in which her characters often find themselves resonates loudly with readers. She is proof that Cape Breton punches *way* above its weight when it comes to producing Canadian writers of really fine prose fiction. There's Alistair MacLeod—who died in 2014, and left a black hole at the centre of Canadian short stories. There's Linden McIntyre, who also won the Giller Prize back in 2009. And then there's Lynn Coady.

For what it's worth, Edmonton doesn't do so badly either. There's Henry Kreisel. And Katherine Govier, who was born in Calgary, but attended the University of Alberta. And, of course, there's Lynn Coady again—a transplanted Cape Bretoner, a true geographer of gender, and a writer who obviously knows this crazy country, quite literally, from coast to coast.

She's here to ask "Who Needs Books?"

PAUL KENNEDY

Edmonton, April 2015

NOTE

1.   Lynn Coady, *Hellgoing: Stories* (Toronto: Astoria, 2013), EPUB edition, 19.

2.   Coady, *Hellgoing*, 112/113.

Who
Needs
Books?

[T]he book is a great technology. There are all these things about it that sound trivial but are immensely important, like as you read a book the *weight* shifts from the unread part of the book to the read part of the book and there's this kind of physical interaction with time passing. When the book is just assumed as the default form of information you don't necessarily ask questions, like what does a page do? What kind of technology is a page? And now I feel like, precisely because it's threatened in some sense, our sense of the book is refreshed...[T]he book is made strange again.

—BEN LERNER

Spare me this melody of life that

disturbs my own music...

—KARL KRAUS

as translated by Jonathan Franzen,
Heine and the Consequences

I love how we talk about
the internet like it isn't us.

—TREI BRUNDRETT

via Twitter

THE MONSTER AT THE END
OF THIS BOOK

THE FIRST BOOK I want to talk about is a book I loved in
childhood. It's not a classic, like *Winnie the Pooh* or Dr. Seuss.
It is much more of pop culture product, a television tie-in
in fact, which is perhaps reflective of the fact that I am very
much a creature of the TV generation. Today's equivalent
might be a book about Dora the Explorer or SpongeBob
SquarePants. In 1969, a children's television show called
Sesame Street debuted and in 1971 Golden Books published
a story that featured the popular program's fuzzy, sad-eyed
character, Grover. It was called *The Monster at the End of
This Book.*

I encountered this book when I was maybe seven or
eight. I had always been a big reader—I owned the collected
Dr. Seuss, the obligatory *Winnie the Pooh*—but this was the
first children's story I had ever come across that was explicitly
interactive. It was like no story I had ever read before—
a commentary on the book itself, beginning with the very
title: *The Monster at the End of This Book*. You opened the cover
and there on the first page was the loveable Grover, terrified.
Wait a minute, he exclaims: did the cover of the book—this
book that he is inside and that you are reading at this very
moment—say what he thinks it did? There's a monster at
the end of the book? But Grover is scared of monsters!

You turn the page and find reality has set in. Grover
grasps that the more pages you turn, the closer you and he
will get to the monster. From here, the book becomes all about
Grover's increasing panic as you, callous child, continue to
gleefully turn pages. Pages 5–6: He binds them with rope.

Pages 9–10: he hammers them together with planks and nails. Pages 13–14: he builds a sturdy brick wall and dares you to try and turn the page now! With each page you turn, the mess you make in Grover's cover-bound world increases along with his frustration and fright. And finally you're there, just one page away from the monster. Who knows what manner of grotesquerie awaits on the other side? Grover begs you to close the book and walk away before all hell breaks lose.

If you're not familiar with the story, you've probably guessed how it ends. It transpires that the harmless and delightful Grover is himself the monster! Our furry, blue narrator is relieved and embarrassed and makes a lame pretence that it was you, not he, who was so terrified all this time. Meanwhile you, the smartypants who suspected the truth all along, close the book with a satisfied chuckle.

As I was gathering my materials for this lecture about books and their assumed endangerment in the digital age, I tried very hard to think of some other way to begin. Some way in besides Grover. Surely there was a salient quote from Marshall McLuhan, or a pithy anecdote from the dawn of the Gutenberg printing press which would better impart the gravitas such a topic deserves. Books are serious after all. At least, in this milieu, the kind of milieu where one might be asked to give a lecture on them, they are seen to be. Notice how I began with an apologetic caveat, that the beloved childhood tome I was about to discuss was not a "classic." That it was from the world of television. For years, many of you will recall, the natural enemy of books in the wilds of modern life was TV. The "idiot box," as it was called, was the brain-killing bogeyman, the dumb, drooling monster that both heralded and awaited us at the end of the book.

But I loved television then, as I love it now. And I'm not kidding when I say I would never have become an author of books without its influence (more on that later). Yet, as a novelist, I've often felt a kind of indirect pressure to toe a certain authorial line. The sense that I should absolutely not begin with a reference to a Muppet, for example. The feeling that writers of novels are obligated to instinctively recoil from the lowbrow excesses of popular culture with its Kim Kardashian Instagram accounts, its hashtags and weasel-riding-woodpecker memes. And what could be more culturally popular, therefore lower-brow, than the furnace in which all these puerile distractions have lately been forged—the internet?

Over the last few decades popular culture and digital media have merged to be considered one and the same. Internet culture is our latest lowbrow bogeyman—the thing "serious" writers feel an indirect pressure to eschew. Unlike the imp of television, which sucked us into its screens, the internet demon possesses the nefarious ability to actively reach out to us, to invade our pockets via iPhones, our ears via earbuds, our minds via the intellectual conduit of keyboards and touch screens. Fifty years ago, worried commenters (often speaking from the decreasing-in-cachet world of newspapers and magazines) could not have imagined a social blight worse than the utterly passive engagement of the iconic "couch potato" TV viewer. But now that passivity has been replaced with the interactive engagement of today's "netizen" (as internet devotees were once quaintly called)—and somehow this transition, from slack-jawed, screen-gazing viewer to slack-jawed, thumb-scrolling web surfer is all the more alarming.

In the face of this rapid cultural shift, many of us in the book trade feel we must remain aloof. Authors, in particular. Aren't we after all the vanguard of what's known as print culture? And isn't print the natural enemy of pixels? Who will defend the printed page—good old-fashioned ink on wood pulp—if not us, the weird, obsessive warriors of the written word? Everyone else involved in publishing is simply doing a job, after all—editors, marketers, booksellers. What does it cost these hardworking souls to make the pragmatic leap from old media into new, once all the deckchairs on the *Titanic* have been thoroughly rearranged? Authors are considered to be a different breed, however. Ours is not a job, but a vocation. We are the captains of the sacred ship, true believers, fully expected—in some corners at least—to go down clinging to our deckchairs.

That is, if you even buy the whole sinking-ship metaphor at all.

Writers, it is insinuated, must inhabit rarefied, pure creative space. Needless to say, the internet with its cat videos and endless varieties of pornography is not that. And these days, such space doesn't make itself as easily available to writers as perhaps it once did—we must claim it when and wherever we can. Novelist Zadie Smith is known to use an app called Anti-Social to force herself offline whenever she needs to work. Barbara Gowdy is rumoured to have two computers in her office positioned against opposite walls—one connected, one not, one for writing, one for surfing. Other writers, like Alberto Manguel, avoid the internet as completely as is possible in modern life. The implication is, we must not pollute our minds with what Jonathan Franzen has called the "yakkers and tweeters" of digital culture.[1] Why? Because we are the gatekeepers, apparently, of a dying yet exalted medium.

Last year, Will Self published a peevishly resigned essay on this very topic called—wait for it—"The Novel is Dead (This Time it's for Real)." In it, he writes:

> [T]he kind of psyche implicit in the production and consumption of serious novels (which are, after all what serious artists produce) depends on a medium that has inbuilt privacy..."[2]

This is what an artist must be at all times: private and serious. *So* serious that the word merits two mentions in this quote alone, and is used seven times in the 4,400-word essay. Yet for all its usage, "serious" is never actually defined—Self does not even make the attempt. He takes its meaning as a given. Quite a lot is taken as a given in this essay.

Yet the more I hear about the need for authors—serious authors at least—to disconnect from mainstream culture as it is currently represented online, the more I think about all the other things it's been hinted to me over the years that serious authors probably shouldn't be caught doing. Certainly, watching television has always been one—if you must, it better be a Ken Burns documentary or a BBC staging of one of Shakespeare's plays. Also suspect: enrolling in a creative writing program at a college or university—because real, serious writers possess a raw and sacred ability that shouldn't be polluted by the tastes and opinions of other people who like to read and write. And certainly, that raw, sacred ability has nothing to do with one's background—say how much one was encouraged to read as a child, how much time one was permitted to devote to one's own writing growing up, how much encouragement one received from one's family and friends. No, some people are simply born

with the innate talent and strength of mind to forge ahead
on their own, and those writers are the ones we call serious.

The other thing writers shouldn't do, it's been insinuated
to me more than once, is hold a job. Because a writer must
write, and nothing else—that's how you can tell he's serious
about it. Certainly it has nothing to do with whether or not
she can afford to even consider the possibility of devoting
herself to writing full time.

I wonder if you see a pattern forming? Me, I see the furry
blue arm of Grover waving in the distance. He's squatting on
a dusty pile of tomes and shouting: Boo!

What is it we're afraid of, exactly? What is the nature
of this end-of-books bogeyman? By referring to it as such,
I suppose I've tipped my hand that I don't believe in it. Let
me give away the ending: I think the monster's Grover. That
is, I think it's just us—not distorted, not grotesque, not made
brainless and cruel and venal by online excess coupled with
aesthetic deprivation. Just us—the way we've always been.

I want to provide a few quotes, just to put things into
perspective:

> I saw that the novel, which at my maturity was the
> strongest and supplest medium for conveying thought
> and emotion from one human being to another, was
> becoming subordinated to a mechanical and communal
> art...capable of reflecting only the tritest thought, the
> most obvious emotion.[3]

This is F. Scott Fitzgerald talking about the medium of film
in 1936. Yet a short time later, film was widely acknowledged
as being well capable of reflecting much more than trite,

obvious thought and emotion, just in a different way than literature did.

But a new cultural blight soon emerged, according to Joyce Carol Oates:

> The television screen, so unlike the movie screen, sharply reduced human beings, revealed them as small, trivial, flat, in two banal dimensions, drained of color. Wasn't there something reassuring about it!...that human beings were merely images...phenomena composed of microscopic flickering dots like atoms.[4]

E.B. White wasn't too fond of television, either:

> If everyone is going to be able to see everything, in the long run all sights may lose whatever rarity value they once possessed, and it may well turn out that people, being able to see and hear practically everything, will be specially interested in almost nothing.[5]

Let's jump back a few centuries. What were people worried about in, say, 1859? Well, one thing they fretted over was

> a pernicious excitement [that] has spread all over the country...[This] is a mere amusement of a very inferior character, which robs the mind of valuable time that might be devoted to nobler acquirements, while at the same time it affords no benefit whatever to the body.[6]

I've heard uncannily similar complaints about video games, but this quote is from an article in *Scientific American* and concerns the game of chess.

And lastly:

[T]his discovery of yours will create forgetfulness in the
learners' souls, because they will not use their memories;
they will trust to the external written characters and not
remember of themselves...they will be hearers of many
things and will have learned nothing; they will appear
to be omniscient and will generally know nothing; they
will be tiresome company, having the show of wisdom
without the reality.[7]

That's Socrates speaking about the written word itself in
Phaedrus, one of Plato's Socratic dialogues, in which he
records a conversation between Phaedrus and Socrates.
This thing we're so anxious to preserve and defend? Socrates
was against it, generally speaking. But he could easily have
been talking about smartphones, particularly with that
thing about people being "tiresome company," appearing
to be omniscient, but generally knowing nothing (Google,
anyone?).

In fact, I selected the quotes above not just because if we
do a mental squint, each could be mistaken for a modern-day
argument against the nefarious aspects of digital culture—it
promotes bad art, it drains us of human empathy, it makes us
dimwitted, obsessive, incurious, lazy and fat. But I also chose
these quotes because when you dig down into the nut of the
anxiety each of these arguments seems to be nurturing, it all
boils down into a single apprehension. That one particular
monster we all fear—and apparently always have feared—
awaits us at the end of the book.

But before we can face that monster, we have to take this
story one page at a time.

GOOD NIGHT, SWEET PRINCE
(OF ART FORMS)

Am I suggesting that books, writing, literature and print culture in general have not been, and are not in the process of being, utterly transformed? I'd be a fool to say so. We all know it's happening, and we're all, to varying degrees, afraid. But what is the exact nature of the terror all this change seems to strike in hearts of book lovers everywhere? This has been my motivating question as I pondered this essay. That we, partakers of reading and writing culture, are afraid, there can be no doubt. I have collected a library of hand-wringing essays on the subject—bemoaning declining attention spans, plummeting book sales, disappearing bookstores, embattled publishing houses. But all of these fears seem to find their ultimate articulation in Will Self's starkly titled piece, so perhaps I'll linger here awhile longer.

The other quality Self invokes with respect to the novel, a quality that goes just as unquestioned as the adjective "serious" is what he calls its "cultural primacy."[8] Self assures us he's not some wild-eyed Chicken Little, he understands that books themselves—that is, long-form fictions published electronically or as a codex—are in no danger. We have publishing juggernauts like J.K. Rowling's "kidult boywizardsroman," as Self calls it, and E.L. James's "soft sadomasochistic porn fantasy" keeping the form afloat. And his vision is not so apocalyptic as to imagine that "serious" books (there's that word again) will one day soon cease to be written and read altogether. The heart of the problem, says Self is that: "[W]hat is…no longer the case is the situation that obtained when I was a young man."

It might be said that we live in an age where a great many not-young men, in a variety of disciplines, are looking around and making the same complaint. But Self's particular point is that in the good old days he is describing, and indeed the second half of the last century, "the literary novel was perceived to be the prince of art forms, the cultural capstone and the apogee of creative endeavour."

This may be true. But he doesn't clarify: perceived by whom?

As literary writer (of the kind of fiction I hope Self would categorize as serious), as a *Canadian* literary writer, as a *female* Canadian literary writer—I had reconciled myself early in my career to the likelihood that my audience would be small—perhaps vanishingly small. This wasn't pessimism. This was pragmatism, a kind of mental vaccine I used to inoculate myself against humiliation and despair. If I couldn't do that, I suspected I'd be left with only two other options: 1) Live in a state of bilious resentment and thwarted entitlement, or 2) Stop writing. This is why I find it difficult to relate to Self's lament about losing the primacy of the novel as an art form, about the novel being stripped of its exalted status in the culture. The culture he's describing—a world where right-thinking people make it their business to seek out the latest acclaimed work of fiction in order to partake of informed, erudite discussions on the topic, and feel appropriately ashamed and left behind if they haven't—was never a given in my life. In what circles has the novel ever been viewed as, as Self defines it: "the cultural capstone and the apogee of creative endeavour"? In some academic circles I suppose. Various urban, artistic enclaves. But certainly none that I was exposed to as a young person. True,

I might be of those circles now, but I grew up desperate to encounter such spaces, had to deliberately seek them out as a young writer and then laboriously set about worming my way into them.

My formative medium, as I mentioned earlier, was television. And the reason I say I would never have become a writer without it, is because I would never have truly grasped that there were people in the world who devoted themselves to writing stories as a vocation if I hadn't seen them on TV. I would never have known about people who made their living as artists. These people didn't exist where I grew up, not as far as I knew, anyway. Similarly, I don't like to think about all the books and films and art and theatre and music I would not have had exposure to without the mere thirteen channels of network television I accessed growing up. Those stations provided a psychic bridge, however rickety, out of my small town on Cape Breton Island and out into the larger world. If I had had access to the internet back then? It makes me dizzy to think how I might have feasted on the culture, literature and art that I so craved. But since I grew up in the pre-digital era, very little of it crossed my transom. Such was not my world.

I might add that when I think about today's version of me—the small-town fourteen-year-old desolately checking out the same books over and over again from the local, bare-bones library—and hear so-called defenders of the culture bemoan, from their home offices in New York and London, her single most accessible portal to the very culture they exalt? I become completely furious on her behalf.

YOU MANIACS!

I'm not suggesting the putative death of the novel, or books, or the written word, is a tragedy only for those of a certain social class. I'm talking about perspective. Ursula K. Le Guin made my point in a much simpler and more elegant fashion in a 2008 essay for *Harper's Magazine* called "Staying Awake: Notes on the Alleged Decline of Reading." Le Guin handily dismisses the allegation early in her piece. "I think," she says, "that [books] are here to stay. It's just that not all that many people ever did read them. Why should we think everybody ought to now?"[9]

Jonathan Franzen made a similar point in a recent interview. Where Self vaguely alludes to a type of book he calls "serious," Franzen zeroes in on perhaps the defining quality Self is hinting at, a quality Franzen calls "moral complexity." He notes:

> People don't want moral complexity. Moral complexity is a luxury. You might be forced to read it in school, but a lot of people have hard lives. They come home at the end of the day, they feel they've been jerked around by the world...the last thing they want to do is read Alice Munro, who is always pointing toward the possibility that you're not the heroic figure you think of yourself as, that you might be the very dubious figure that other people think of you as. You want to be told *good people are good, bad people are bad, and love conquers all.*[10]

For those of us steeped, and who have steeped ourselves, in literary culture, this can feel like a harsh truth. The fact is, most people don't read, and the ones who do by and large are not picking up the books you and I and Franzen and Self might prescribe. Today's new Jamesians (I'm referring to E.L., of *50 Shades of Grey* fame) outnumber the old Jamesians (by which I mean Henry—remember him?) to an extent upon which I'd prefer not to dwell. But it's a truth we must face up to if we presume to take the podium in a lecture hall, or in the pages of a major newspaper or an online webmag and proclaim something as sweeping, vague and essentially dubious as the end of books. (As an aside: around the time I was revising this essay, the *50 Shades of Grey* trilogy dominated the top three spots in the *Washington Post's* list of current bestsellers.)

In fact, despite the ongoing elegizing of media pundits and commentators, assuring us that everything book culture represents—reading, literacy, imagination, empathy and human communication—is going the way of the independent bookstore, recent numbers from the publishing industry demonstrate that overall book sales are relatively stable, and that consumers are reading as much as ever. This despite mass bookstore closures, a publishing industry locked in perpetual battle with the Amazon goliath, dwindling book review sections in newspapers and, of course, dwindling newspapers themselves. So even though we look around and feel as if book culture as we know it is crumbling to dust, there's one important thing to keep in mind: the key phrase here is *as we know it.*

Meanwhile you might be thinking: *Pshaw*, sales numbers. Where's the moral complexity in that? Sure, *Gone Girl* and the latest Stephen King are going great guns, just as they always have, but the crass, bottom-line logic of the marketing department is not what's at the heart of Self and Franzen's respective laments. Still, when it comes to Self's argument in particular, I find myself increasingly suspicious of the condition he diagnoses as "death" when it comes to the novel, of how adeptly he blurs the lines between obliteration and what he refers to as the novel's loss of "cultural primacy." A close reading of his essay—much of which I agree with— reveals that he's not elegizing the novel at all, but its *status*. And not its status according to just anyone, but its status as understood by a small demographic of people like himself, people who are deeply invested in the idea of the novel, and books themselves, as artefacts utterly essential to our cultural well-being. And if the declining status of the novel is indeed a symptom of our aesthetic culture withering into oblivion, what do you suppose it is that's making us sick? No surprise, it's the world of digitally driven bugs, worms and virality—the internet.

This brings us to Self's coup de grâce. Say we accept the premises I question above, say we all agree on a thing called a "serious novel" which has for decades enjoyed "cultural primacy and centrality."[11] If we're agreed on that, and if we're Pollyanna enough to believe that this primacy and centrality will endure over the coming decades, Self has one final question for us:

> [I]f you accept that by then the vast majority of text will be read in digital form on devices linked to the web, do you also believe that those readers will voluntarily choose to disable that connectivity? If your answer to this is no, then the death of the novel is sealed from your own mouth.

Sealed from our own mouths! We've done it to ourselves, like at the end of *Planet of the Apes*, when Charlton Heston escapes his simian captors only to discover he's not on another planet at all, but on earth, centuries in the future. "You maniacs! You blew it up!" he declares. By *you*, of course, Heston means we. He can't escape the destruction his clueless, technophile human brethren have wrought, and nor can we. We've constructed our own digital prisons, handed the keys to the damn dirty ape inhabitants of Silicon Valley and sacrificed the one thing that could have liberated us: books, the apogee of creative endeavour.

I don't know. I don't know what a "serious novel" is exactly and I don't know if I buy its supposed "cultural primacy" and I don't know if in the future most of the reading we'll be doing will take place on devices connected to the web. But let's say that last bit at least is true. Self doesn't say "all" reading, but "most," and that seems likely. Have I just sealed the death of the novel by saying so? I don't believe so.

Self seems to be positing that there will be so much fun stuff available on these electronic devices that people won't opt to read nearly as much as they do now. Yes they will be reading books, just not very often. But, see, that's not death—he's still just talking about status. And something doesn't seem to have occurred to him—isn't it likely that the popularity of these devices and their ubiquity might actually lead to an expanded reading demographic? More people play games than read books. More people watch porn than read books. More people watch sports and TV and movies than read books. As Ursula K. Le Guin has already pointed out, it has ever been thus. Le Guin has a much more realistic view of the reading population than Self does—we "serious" readers comprise a small demographic who, unlike the majority, *love* to read. We don't consider it a kind of cultural medicine we're obligated to take. It's not a chore, something to be forced on recalcitrant children like broccoli. We are fetishists, "hedonists," according to Le Guin, members of the small, proud tribe who read books, and always will— "because we want to." "Were such people ever in the majority?" Le Guin asks, rhetorically, because we all know the answer.[12]

So isn't there a chance that if you give people a device that allows them to pursue the recreations and distractions that people have always pursued anyway, *in addition* to the opportunity to easily download and read books, what you may very well end up with is more people than ever reading books? After all, there are no bookstands at hockey arenas. If you go to see *Gone Girl* or *The Hobbit* at the movie theatre, no one is going to offer you a copy of the book when you emerge after the credits roll. But with all our entertainments rolled up into a single device, isn't it at least possible that books could reach an audience they've never reached before?

Ah, but even then, perhaps these books that the coming cyborg generation end up reading would not be "serious" enough to please Will Self. In which case I would reassure him that his so-called serious readers, Le Guin's hedonists— those of us who read because it is our passion and obsession—are not going anywhere. Modern life has tried to discourage us at every turn—called us nerds, weirdos, mousy-librarian-types, pussies, poindexters—and we have resolutely dug in our heels. You may not find these readers at a hockey arena or a screening of *Gone Girl*, but there's one place they will always reliably turn up: At your doorstep, Mr. Author, waiting patiently.

BUT WHAT ABOUT
THE CHILDREN?

Noted tech-buff and icon of "serious" literature, Margaret Atwood, is one of the few authors of her generation who has seamlessly embraced the new digital technologies and is almost singular in her refusal to rend her clothes and lament the end of literary culture. She has gone on the record as dismissing the dual-bugbears that 1) young people aren't reading and 2) traditional publishing is doomed, with a distinctly unruffled shrug. Writing in *The Guardian*, she reflects on being scolded for having said so:

> I got into trouble a while ago for saying that I thought the internet led to increased literacy—people scolded me about the shocking grammar to be found online—but I was talking about fundamentals: quite simply, you can't use the net unless you can read. Reading and writing, like everything else, improve with practice. And, of course, if there are no young readers and writers, there will shortly be no older ones."[13]

This is an important point. Every time I hear someone bemoan the smartphone generation—specifically, how you can't go into a coffee shop or ride a streetcar without being confronted by a horde of inattentive screen-zombies staring at their phones, I always wonder if it has never occurred to the bemoaner how many of these people are reading. After all, online video is always only video, but the variety of reading we can do online is endless. You can read texts, emails, *The New Yorker* (which has a splendidly designed

app for this purpose), newspapers, Twitter, Facebook and—
yes—books. I recall a similar complaint in the 1980s when
the social blight du jour was the Walkman, which prompted
the phenomenon of young people wearing headphones
in public, deliberately cutting themselves off from the
outside world. But, I remember thinking, what's wrong with
listening to music everywhere you go?

Atwood goes on to reflect on how one of the co-founders
of Wattpad (an online, free reading and writing platform
with an international subscribership in the millions), told
her about receiving a letter from an old man in a village in
Africa. The village, she wrote, "had no school, no library, no
landline, and no books. But it had a mobile phone, and on
that they could read and share the Wattpad stories. He was
writing to say thank you."[14]

This is a startling and counterintuitive anecdote when
you consider the fact that only 40 per cent of the world's
population has access to the internet—something we in the
western world generally chide ourselves to keep in mind
when we discuss the influence of digital culture. But how
exhilarating to think that a village with no access to any
of the traditional institutions of literacy—schools, books,
libraries—can have its isolation and lack of resources so
mitigated by a single piece of online technology.

Here are a few quick, recent findings from the publishing
world and its attendants that bolster Atwood's point. In
September 2014, a Pew survey of more than six thousand
Americans found that millennials—that's right, twenty-
somethings, the demographic who essentially exited the
womb with smartphones in hand—have been reading more
books than people over thirty.[15]

This past January, the British Library released a report observing with an air of pleasant surprise a 10 per cent rise in visitor numbers over the previous twelve months. It noted that the world of "increasingly digital and screen-based knowledge" seems not to have led not to a diminishing interest in physical libraries, but just the opposite. "The more screen-based our lives, it seems," read the report, "the greater the perceived value of real human encounters and physical artefacts: activity in each realm feeds interest in the other."[16]

Furthermore, research presented at the Neilsen Children's Book Summit in December 2014 reported that today's children and teenagers are reading in record numbers. The children's book market has grown 44 per cent in the last ten years, and international children's publishing is the largest sector of content creation at $151 billion, surpassing even *gaming*.[17]

The summit's keynote speaker was Harvard's Rey Junco, who researches young people and social media at the Berkman Center for Internet and Society. His studies have found that not only do 67 per cent of today's teens spend their leisure time reading, but 50 per cent of them say they prefer print books over e-books. Junco found that, contrary to the assumption of older generations, the online activity of young people that we declaim for its supposed shallow obsessiveness hasn't actually debased their social, intellectual or emotional skills in any measurable way— in some respects it seems to have increased them.

So this problem we're having with the internet? This problem of waning attention spans and distraction and never having any time to read? It would appear to be mostly our problem—an issue for the generation author Mark Prensky, writing in 2001, dubbed "digital immigrants"—

those of us who exist with one foot in the world of old media and one in the new.[18] But the kids, the digital natives, it would appear, are all right, or at the very least, no worse off than before—surfing, gaming, hanging out both online and off. And reading in greater numbers than ever. The problems they do seem to be having with regard to technology—TMI tweets and Facebook posts, cyberbullying, the ill-advised sharing of sexually explicit photos—seem very much the kind of challenges that arise when a generation native to a new technology lacks a generation of elders who have travelled this terrain before. A generation who can offer guidance based on long experience. We're not it.

THE END OF CIVILIZATION
AS WE KNOW IT

This would not be the first time in history an older demographic has projected its anxieties and fears about the way the world is changing onto its youth. In his book on writing, *The Sense of Style: The Thinking Person's Guide to Writing in the 21st Century*, linguist Steven Pinker asserts that every generation thinks the one coming up behind it heralds the end of civilization as we know it.[19] We fear what they will do to the institutions we cherish the way new parents fear for their beloved heirlooms and photographs, placing them ever higher out of a toddler's rampaging reach.

In his book, however, Pinker does not for one minute allow readers to get away with the assumption that modernity has destroyed the written word, or that the language skills of young people are any more debased than those of the generation that came before them. He's so emphatic, I suspect this widespread misapprehension is a pet peeve of his. In an interview with *Scientific American*, Pinker noted:

> Studies of writing quality in student papers have shown that there has been no deterioration over the decades, and no, today's college students don't substitute smiley-faces and texting abbreviations for words and phrases.[20]

When I was seeking feedback on this essay, one reader suggested to me that making a statement like the above in a room full of professional educators who likely have to deal with student writing every day could potentially incite a riot. So I just want to assure you I contacted Steven Pinker. I asked him to point me to the specific studies suggesting that, indeed, there has been no deterioration of student writing over the decades, and he did. The general finding seems to be that while today's students make *different* written errors than their pre-digital counterparts (spellcheck being one of the more obvious reasons), the overall number of errors itself has not changed.

In his book, Pinker adds:

> As people age, they confuse changes in themselves with changes in the world, and changes in the world with moral decline—the illusion of the good old days.[21]

He then offers up an entertaining array of greybeard lamentations over the decades and centuries concerning the woefully decaying standards of reading and writing in the young.

From 1978: "The common language is disappearing..."[22]

From 1961: "They cannot construct a simple declarative sentence, either orally or in writing..."[23]

From 1917: "Our freshman can't spell, can't punctuate... every high school is in disrepair because its pupils are so ignorant of the merest rudiments."[24]

From 1785: "Our language is degenerating very fast..."[25]

From 1478, from William Caxton soon after he set up the first printing press in England: "Certaynly our langage now vsed veryeth ferre from what whiche was vsed and spoken when I was borne."[26]

Finally Pinker notes that according to certain scholars there exist clay tablets written in ancient Sumerian that "include complaints about the deteriorating writing skills of the young."[27]

All of this is to suggest, I suppose, that reading and writing and everything it represents to the culture—literacy, intellectual depth, human engagement—aren't dead, they are just perpetually in decline...in the shared imagination of people like ourselves. People whose lives are so profoundly sustained by literacy, by the joy of reading, that we can't quite allow ourselves to believe it won't be taken away from us. It seems safer somehow to throw up our hands in pre-emptive surrender, a tactic born of defeatism—like breaking up with the boyfriend we adore because we're so certain he'll do it to us the moment we let our guard down.

This counterintuitive eagerness of the book's most passionate adherents to bury and praise it simultaneously reminds me of a section in Michael Harris's recent book, an elegy for the pre-internet age called *The End of Absence: Reclaiming What We've Lost in a World of Constant Connection*. In it, he describes a character in the Victor Hugo novel *Notre*

Dame de Paris, set in 1482 when the Gutenberg printing press was just beginning to establish a foothold in France.

> Archdeacon Claude Frollo sees his first printed book and marvels/glowers at its production quality. He stands near Notre-Dame and, looking up at the cathedral, says, "This will kill that."[28]

Further down the page, Harris imagines a version of the scenario for the digital age. An internet-addled citizen of the twenty-first century stands in Times Square, looking up from an iPad to behold the New York Times building, "where," Harris remarks, "hundreds of positions have been cut in recent years..." The iPad wielder thinks to herself, echoing Frollo, "This kills that."[29] It's a nice analogy. There's only one thing that niggles at me. Notre Dame Cathedral is still standing. And it's no relic of an ancient, dead belief, like Stonehenge or the Parthenon. Catholicism still exists. It's different, yes. It's changed radically over the centuries— yet, in some ways, hardly at all. But the religious fervour, architectural vision and sheer human ingenuity that gave rise to the gothic glories of Notre Dame Cathedral haven't gone anywhere.

Is *The New York Times*, and newspaper culture as we know it—there's that phrase again: *as we know it*—dying? Arguably. Just as the Catholic Church as it was understood in France in the late 1400s could have been said to be "dying" in the wake of the printing press. Without question, traditional news-rooms have been floundering these past two or so decades, as many prominent journalists have observed. But some of those observers will also often describe the current era in the

very same breath as a journalistic golden age. In a recent
piece where he advised young writers to divest themselves of
any hope of a career in journalism, Felix Salmon in the next
paragraph declared himself a "golden-ager," writing

> I'm constantly astonished by the quantity and quality of
> the material being produced today...and I think this is
> probably the greatest era for journalism that the world
> has ever seen.[30]

So superlative journalism is still being written, and published.
But the business model that has nurtured it up until this
moment is in the process of transforming itself—indeed we
might say dying—in order to make way for something else.
To perhaps a less obvious extent, the same is true of book
publishing.

One of the frustrations of a notorious 2013 essay by
Jonathan Franzen called "What's Wrong with the Modern
World" is the fact that he combines an acute grasp of the
dangers of what he calls "technoconsumerism"—what I
would simply call modern capitalism—with a too-broad
dismissal of digital culture itself.[31] One moment he is
thrillingly declaiming against the faux-humanistic rhetoric
of technoconsumerism and how it "abets the frank mono-
polism of the techno-titans," and the next he is grumping
like someone's misanthropic uncle about how hard it is to
get through a meal without "somebody reaching for an
iPhone." One moment he is denouncing the rapacious
business practices of Amazon—which I would agree are
perilously monopolistic—but in the next manages to
besmirch "yakkers and tweeters," the innumerable readers
and writers who, unlike himself, enjoy using social media—

what he calls "intolerably shallow forms of social engagement." You'd think we were all a bunch of Dorothy Parkers and Bernard Shaws pre-internet, swanning from one salon to the next, our every social interaction replete with equal parts wit and profundity. Banal small talk, gossip and chit-chat never existed.

What happens, Franzen asks, pleading from the ruins of the bombed-out New York Public Library (or so I imagine him)

> to the people who want to communicate in depth, individual to individual, in the quiet and permanence of the printed word, and who were shaped by their love of writers who wrote when publication still assured some kind of quality control and literary reputations were more than a matter of self-promotional decibel levels?[32]

What happens indeed? Well, for one thing, in Jonathan Franzen's case anyway, he gets put on the cover of *Time* magazine and declared the greatest writer in America.

Again, I'm asking for a little perspective. I sympathize with literary purists like Franzen, who have, over the past twenty or so years, witnessed tectonic shifts in the publishing industry. I understand how it can seem like the people who rode out these shifts most successfully are not the next generation of Jonathan Franzens (whatever that might look like) but authors such as Franzen's personal bête noire, Jennifer Weiner, a bestselling writer of frothy "women's fiction" and prodigious Twitter-user. But Franzen's lament above makes it sound as if he thinks novelists of Weiner's stripe were rare before the digital age, and certainly never reliably out-sold their more "serious" counterparts.

It might be true that the internet has allowed a stunning profusion of self-published work to appear in our midst— work that is often exuberantly, even defiantly, illiterate, ungrammatical and unedited. But as Margaret Atwood observed in a 2013 interview, there has always been what we might call bad, or at the very least "unserious," writing:

> Out of the Gutenberg printing presses poured lots of pornography, which we decided to forget. The classics are just the part of the iceberg that is still visible. The point is, when you make things more accessible and visible as they are on the Web, it doesn't make things a lot worse. It's just all in front of you, and you can see it."[33]

Novelist Kurt Vonnegut liked to brag that one of his proudest achievements was the day his novel *Slaughterhouse-Five* knocked Jacqueline Susann, author of *Valley of the Dolls* (arguably the *50 Shades* of its time) off the bestseller list after her novel *The Love Machine* reigned there for over a year. Not because he considered his work so much more impressive, but because he understood how extraordinary and rare an achievement it is when a work of "serious" literature achieves the sales numbers of your average work of soft-core titillation. Or your average spy thriller. Or YA wizard novel. Here is the eternal truth about the reading public: we'll choose the Susanns and the Weiners over the Vonneguts and Franzens nine times out of ten. But no one's denied the Vonneguts and Franzens their turn at the top of the bestseller lists, and the internet has not forged a new demographic of techno-philistines, turning up their noses at any book that doesn't have a vampire on the cover. It's like Atwood says—the benign philistinism of the public just happens to be more apparent to us now thanks to this new window the internet provides, with its occasionally uncomfortable view on the great, unwashed reading and writing masses. By way of example, one of the biggest success stories of Amazon's self-publishing program is an author called Virginia Wade, who was able to put her daughter through college thanks to the success of her wildly popular series of "bigfoot erotica" called, forgive me, *Cum for Bigfoot*, volumes 1 through 5.

TECHNOSERFS

The problem with this conversation we've been having over the past couple of decades is that it perpetually confuses capitalism with technology and technology with culture itself. Technology exists apart from, but is profoundly influenced by, capitalism, and the same can be said of culture. And just because our still-new technologies are currently having a profound impact on our culture, doesn't mean our culture would be any better or worse off without them—it would simply be another version of itself.

If books truly are imperilled—and now I'm talking about "books" according to Self and Franzen's implicit definition, which I take to mean culturally significant works of narrative literary art—we need to bring a little clarity and a lot less alarmism to the table. Franzen in his essay moves seamlessly between lamenting Apple and Amazon's corporate practices to disparaging "tweeters" as if, rhetorically, this doesn't amount to complaining about a rabbit you just tripped over in the course of fleeing Godzilla and King Kong. It's easy to look at young people with their fingers dancing across their iPhones and tell ourselves they are somehow ruining society just by being more proficient than we are at using the very technology we have placed in their hands. It's less easy to blame a diffuse group of people who hold a great deal of power and can sometimes make bad decisions about what we get to read and how we get to read it. It's also easy to talk about how "the internet" killed "the bookstore"—cultural commentators have been doing a lot of that in the past decade. But the internet didn't kill the bookstore. It was something called business as usual. The *independent* bookstore was killed off first, by big box retailers. They, in turn, were killed off by Amazon.com. The cultural shift this represents sounds a lot less tragic and romantic put in terms of one massive corporate entity being elbowed into irrelevance by another.

The degree to which the internet can feel like an unwelcome and nefarious intrusion into our lives depends in large part on the way we use it—and, more importantly, the way it's used against us (deliberately or not) by the people in charge. In a 2008 essay called "Is Google Making us Stupid," Nicholas Carr compares the internet's reshaping of our lives and cognitive functions to the way the invention of the clock habituated us to think and function according to the dictates of its hands.[34] This, he suggests, paved the way for the dehumanizing strictures of the industrial age and the eventual treatment of human workers as automatons. Of course, the clock itself didn't actually do that. The industrial age was the result of business and factory owners rejoicing in a technology they understood would allow them to measure and exploit worker efficiency down to the very second.

Early in his book, *The End of Absence*, Michael Harris describes how the imposition of social media essentially forced him out of a job. As an editor at *Vancouver Magazine* in 2008, Harris describes a typical day at his desk, being besieged by the constant opening of iChat windows, beeping email alerts and pinging text messages. "At one point in that harried afternoon," he writes, "I stop and count the number of windows open on my two monitors. Fourteen. As I count them up, my phone pings again and I look down at the text message glowing there: *Dude are you alive or what?*"[35]

It's this disgruntled text from a neglected friend that finally awakens Harris from his technocratic slumber. Soon after, he quits his job.

I remember magazine culture in 2008—this was a bad time for publishing culture in general. It was the year of the crash, don't forget, and publishing was more desperate than ever to figure out how to turn the prodigious gifts of online technology to its own bottom-line advantage, lest it should end up a cautionary tale like the decimated music industry became. It must've seemed only natural, back then, that a dedicated labourer in the salt mines of the magazine industry would want and need to be in ongoing real-time contact with his peers and colleagues. But now that we've spent a few more years getting to know these online tools, I think we can all agree how ludicrous it is to suppose anyone could ever get any dedicated work done with our phone notifications turned on and our instant messenger clients open in the background. In his recent book, *The Organized Mind: Thinking Straight in the Age of Information Overload*, neuroscientist Daniel Levitin describes digital media's effects on our brains in terms of the ways in which we allow it to distract us—emphasis on *allow*.[36] When we're constantly interrupted by pings and notifications, our brains attempt to multitask and our efficiency, memory and productivity suffers. But our brain isn't being somehow irrevocably damaged by exposure to digital media itself, it's simply being pulled in multiple directions at once. Fortunately, it's within our power to mitigate that distraction—we simply turn off our notifications and, when necessary, we unplug.

So this moment of reckoning Harris describes in his book is not some Neo-in-the-Matrix awakening, an unambiguous example of technology having wrested away one man's human reality. No, it's just one of many examples of the clumsy, inefficient application of technology by a workplace that still hasn't figured out the best way to make use of it. If it isn't yet clear, I'm saying the internet can feel like such a rude imposition on our lives, like a yoke, because capitalism uses it that way. Capitalism has always imposed the latest technology onto workers in less than benign ways—the clock being one obvious example, the camera another. After all, a yoke is just a harmless piece of wood—until the moment someone places it on our backs.

My point is, let's keep our eye on the ball here. If you have all the free time in the world and you spend it on Facebook, ok, that's a problem—Mark Zuckerberg has clearly worked his dark mojo on you. But if you spend every spare moment frantically fielding tweets, texts and emails because your employer requires nothing less, that's another. Think about who, and what exactly, in either of these scenarios, is stopping you from picking up a book.

WE HAPPY FEW

I suspect if you're reading this, you count yourself as one of the lucky ones who does have the time and attention to read, and is grateful for that advantage. If you've picked up this book, you are a reader, a devotee of the written word—a member of Le Guin's small tribe of hedonists.

So now I'd like to talk about us hedonists and this thing that unites us—the book. Exactly why is it we like it so much, and what are we getting out of it?

In late 2014 when I was beginning to think about writing this lecture, feeling cowed and panicked at how many pages it would have to be, and how long I would have to stand talking in front of an audience when the time came to deliver it, and the multitude of ways my arguments could likely be picked apart, not to mention the fact that I didn't even quite know yet what my arguments were—I had a great idea. I decided to go on Twitter.

At the time I had a little over 5,000 followers. As a side note: the month before, my followers hovered around 4,000, but then former CBC radio host Jian Ghomeshi, in a notorious Facebook post, referenced a short story I wrote as part of an argument in defense of what he claimed were his harmless sexual predilections. And in the wake of the sex abuse scandal his post kicked off, my follower count shot up—which needless to say I had mixed feelings about. So you see that Jonathan Franzen's not the only one—I too have had my struggles with social media.

But thus far Twitter had been more friend than antagonist to me, and I knew many of my followers were passionate readers. So I decided to conduct an informal poll. I asked

my friends on Twitter—those who specifically identified
themselves as book lovers—to describe to me what exactly
the quality of the experience of reading a book was that they
so loved?

I have to tell you, I was honestly not expecting that so
many of the people who replied—these dedicated users of
social media—would speak unprompted and with such
reverence and affection about the tactile pleasures of the
physical book itself. I was expecting lofty descriptions of
purely intellectual experiences. Communion with the
writer's mind. Immersion in imaginary worlds. Absorption
in language. And I did get that. But I got just as much, if
not more, rhapsodizing on qualities like *smell*. The texture
of pages beneath the fingers. The creak of a fresh binding
being broken. And it wasn't just the physicality of the book
itself that was lauded. Often it was the physical pleasures
surrounding the *ritual* of reading a book. People talked about
the beverages they like to have on hand when they read.
The weight of a new stack in a bag, being carried home from
the bookstore. The satisfaction of seeing them lined up on a
shelf, waiting to be read. The physical activity of "curling up"
with a book was evoked multiple times.

I have to admit I went into the poll thinking on some
level that the idea that readers need and want physical
books in large part for their very object-ness was mostly
a Franzenesque sentimentality for the way reading has
traditionally been done. I've thought better since then. I now
understand that readers' enthusiasm for the physicality of
books isn't about romance, it's about pleasure itself. And
it's about mental health, in the way that most pleasure is.
Human beings are sensual creatures. We like *things*—objects
we can touch, smell and hear. Screens have given us much,

but swiping right and left is not a particularly sensual experience.

And that leads me to point out the fear that I believe is central to what we collectively imagine to be the monster awaiting us at the end of the book. A fear that soon the temptations of technology will become so alluring, we'll forgo our humanity and all its physical pleasures and encumbrances altogether. It's a nonsensical fear of course, but its as old, if not older, than the printed word. It's the fear behind all our favourite science fictions, after all—from *Planet of the Apes* to the *Terminator* franchise to the Spike Jonze film *Her*. You might say, the fear of relinquishing our humanity is as human as anything else about us.

Do you know what else is human, though? Distraction. Play. Procrastination. Farting around. Checking out. And feeling guilty about it. The fact that so many of us put digital technology to these unproductive uses is no more damning than the fact that we in large part do the same— and always have—with more traditional media. I never really understood what Marshall McLuhan meant when he asserted we don't read a newspaper, we get into it like a warm bath, until I owned an iPad. McLuhan, I realized, was talking about the medium his generation used to mentally check out, and I was feeling the truth of his statement as I sat with the medium I most often used for the same purpose.

Many of those my age and older will likely remember the iconic image from the good old days, of a traditional '50s-era patriarch in a room with his nagging wife and noisy children, serenely blocking them out with the day's newspaper held up in front of his face. Whenever I think about today's so-called blight of people on trains and buses staring at their phones, defiantly ignoring one another, I recall a wonderful photograph by a young Stanley Kubrick, taken on the New York subway in the mid-forties. Every single passenger has a newspaper in front of their face. My point is, urbanites didn't want to deal with one another then anymore than they do now. I don't believe there ever was a golden age of constant nodding, smiling and tipping one's hat. Riding the bus can be a misery. Walking down the street. can be a tedium. Dealing with other people can be exhausting. Sometimes you just want to bury your head in a newspaper or watch YouTube or listen to a podcast. That is as human as anything else. As is writing a poem, or singing an aria, or just enjoying a really wonderful face-to-face conversation with someone whose company you actually desire.

In my Twitter poll, when people weren't talking about smell and feel they were talking about something else—the intellectual experience. They described a craving for the sense of immersion that reading gives them. Some people spoke of it as a kind of psychological privacy, no matter where they happened to be. More than one person used the word "escape." Here, I believe, is where the book truly does have the advantage over the internet. The internet gives us a sense of communication, as does the book. And similar to the book, it offers up a means of "checking out" from time to time—a warm bath of narrative in which to immerse ourselves. But what it doesn't and can never offer really is a sense of complete and total privacy. Of psychic escape. When you hear about people announcing that they need to "unplug" for a weekend or conduct a "social media cleanse" or take a "Facebook break," we understand what they are fleeing—the cacophony, the very connectedness that makes the internet such a revolutionary and seductive phenomenon.

But the utter mental absorption we experience when we read a written narrative, the way the world disappears around us and an entirely imaginary place springs to life in our consciousness, is unparalleled and impossible to replicate with any other medium. Reading is dreaming awake—Kurt Vonnegut called it the "western version of meditation." The internet may give us immersion, and it may give us community, but what it can never give us is this experience of dreaming in tandem with an individual author's imagination. Only books do that.

The fact that some of us prefer to enact this with a sheaf of printed pages between two bound covers, and some would rather use a Kindle or Kobo doesn't make that experience any less magical, or less singular. Here is why, according to author Rebecca Solnit:

> The object we call a book is not the real book, but its potential, like a musical score or seed. It exists fully only in the act of being read; and its real home is inside the head of the reader, where the symphony resides, the seed germinates. A book is a heart that beats only in the chest of another.[37]

The desire readers have for this singular, magical experience, no matter what kind of technology provides it to them, is, I assure you, never going away. It will certainly never be willingly *relinquished*, as people like Will Self seem to fear, traded for a mess of digital pottage. As if Candy Crush and BuzzFeed listicles and the latest Spider-Man reboot could ever replace what books provide. Twitter can be enormously diverting, but no one's ever going to describe a tweet, no matter how cleverly phrased, as "a heart that beats only in the chest of another."

So here we are at the end of the book and much to Grover's relief, and despite the mess he made in all his panic, not that much has changed. And if there's one message Grover and I would like you to take away with you it's this: Fear not. Technology does not have the power to alter our most profound human yearnings and experiences. How do I know that? Because in all of human history, it never has.

Books are not going away any more than family is going away, any more than community is going away, any more than love and intellectual inquiry are ever going away. Poetry is never going away—and yes, it's important to keep these two ideas in your head at the same time: 1) hardly anyone reads poetry and 2) poetry has always existed.

The human love affair with narrative is certainly never going away, nor are the spiritual and aesthetic experiences of truth and beauty that we happy few have always sought via reading. People like us—book lovers, hedonists—we're part of every generation, and I can't believe we will ever cease to seek out the singular experience that books provide. It's too rare, too valuable, and most significantly, its adherents are some of the most passionate and devoted people I know.

NOTES

1. Jonathan Franzen,"What's Wrong With the Modern World," *The Guardian*, 13 September 2013, https://web.archive.org/web/20130915070641/http://www.theguardian.com/books/2013/sep/13/jonathan-franzen-wrong-modern-world.

2. Will Self, "The Novel is Dead (This Time It's for Real)," *The Guardian*, 2 May 2014, http://www.theguardian.com/books/2014/may/02/will-self-novel-dead-literary-fiction.

3. F. Scott Fitzgerald and James L.W. West, *My Lost City: Personal Essays, 1920–1940* (Cambridge: Cambridge University Press, 2005), EPUB edition, 148.

4. Joyce Carol Oates, *You Must Remember This* (New York: Dutton, 1987), 122.

5. E.B. White, *Writings from The New Yorker 1927–1976* (New York: HarperCollins, 1990), 175.

6. "Chess-Playing Excitement," *Scientific American [New Series]* 1, no. 1 (2 July 1859), 9.

7. Plato, *Phaedrus*, trans. Benjamin Jowett (s.l: n.p: 1997), EPUB edition, 200.

8. Self, "The Novel is Dead."

9. Ursula K. Le Guin, "Staying Awake: Notes on the Alleged Decline of Reading," *Harper's Magazine*, February 2008, http://harpers.org/archive/2008/02/staying-awake/.

10. Susan Lerner, "A Conversation with Jonathan Franzen," *Booth: A Journal*, 3 February 2015, http://booth.butler.edu/2015/02/13/a-conversation-with-jonathan-franzen/.

11. Self, "The Novel is Dead."

12. Le Guin, "Staying Awake," 37.

13. Margaret Atwood, "Why Wattpad Works," *The Guardian*, 6 July 2012, http://www.theguardian.com/books/2012/jul/06/margaret-atwood-wattpad-online-writing.

14. Atwood, "Why Wattpad Works."

15. Kathryn Zickuhr and Lee Rainie, "Younger Americans and Public Libraries," *Pew Research Center*, 10 September 2014, http://www.pewinternet.org/files/2014/09/PI_YoungerAmericansandLibraries_091014.pdf.

16. The British Library Board, *Living Knowledge: The British Library 2015–2023*, n.d., 8. http://www.bl.uk/aboutus/foi/pubsch/pubscheme3/living-knowledge-2015-2023.pdf.

17. Erin L. Cox, "Forget Your Preconceptions About Teenagers and Reading," *Publishing Perspectives*, 16 December 2014, http://publishingperspectives.com/2014/12/forget-preconceptions-teenagers-reading/#.Vju_yqIlvaQ.

18. Cox, "Forget Your Preconceptions."

19. Steven Pinker, *The Sense of Style: The Thinking Person's Guide to Writing in the 21st Century* (New York: Viking, 2014): 16.

20. Gareth Cook, "Steven Pinker's Sense of Style," *Scientific American*, 30 September 2014, http://www.scientificamerican.com/article/steven-pinker-s-sense-of-style/.

21. Pinker, *The Sense of Style*, 16.

22. Pinker, *The Sense of Style*, 16.

23. Pinker, *The Sense of Style*, 17.

24. Pinker, *The Sense of Style*, 17.

25. Pinker, *The Sense of Style*, 17.

26. Pinker, *The Sense of Style*, 17.

27. Pinker, *The Sense of Style*, 17.

28. Michael Harris, *The End of Absence: Reclaiming What We've Lost in a World of Constant Connection* (s.l.: HarperCollins, 2014), EPUB edition, 21.

29. Harris, *The End of Absence*, 21.

30. Felix Salmon, "To All the Young Journalists Asking for Advice," *Fusion*, 9 February 2015, http://fusion.net/story/45832/to-all-the-young-journalists-asking-for-advice/.

31. Franzen, "What's Wrong with the Modern World."

32. Franzen, "What's Wrong with the Modern World."

33. Sarah Lacy, "'Every Time Technology Changes, It Changes What People in the Plot Can Do.' An Interview With Margaret Atwood," *Pando*, 30 August 2012, https://pando.com/2012/08/30/every-time-technology-changes-it-changes-what-people-in-the-plot-can-do-an-interview-with-margaret-atwood/.

34. Nicholas Carr, "Is Google Making Us Stupid? What the Internet Is Doing to Our Brains," *The Atlantic*, July/August 2008,

http://www.theatlantic.com/magazine/archive/2008/07/is-google-making-us-stupid/306868/.

35.   Harris, *The End of Absence*, 12.

36.   Daniel J. Levitin, *The Organized Mind: Thinking Straight in the Age of Information Overload* (New York: Dutton, 2014), 96.

37.   Rebecca Solnit, *The Faraway Nearby* (s.l.: Penguin Group US, 2013), EPUB edition, 51.

BIBLIOGRAPHY

Atwood, Margaret. "Why Wattpad Works." *The Guardian*, 6 July 2012.
http://www.theguardian.com/books/2012/jul/06/margaret-atwood-
wattpad-online-writing.

The British Library Board. *Living Knowledge: The British Library 2015–2023*.
n.d. http://www.bl.uk/aboutus/foi/pubsch/pubscheme3/living-
knowledge-2015-2023.pdf.

Carr, Nicholas. "Is Google Making Us Stupid? What the Internet Is Doing
to Our Brains." *The Atlantic*, July/August 2008. http://www.theatlantic.
com/magazine/archive/2008/07/is-google-making-us-stupid/306868/.

"Chess-Playing Excitement." *Scientific American [New Series]* 1, no. 1 (2 July
1859).

Coady, Lynn. *Hellgoing: Stories*. Toronto, ON: Astoria, 2013. EPUB edition.

Cox, Erin L. "Forget Your Preconceptions About Teenagers and Reading."
Publishing Perspectives, 16 December 2014.
http://publishingperspectives.com/2014/12/forget-preconceptions-
teenagers-reading/#.Vju_yqIlvaQ.

Fitzgerald, F. Scott and James L.W. West. *My Lost City: Personal Essays, 1920–
1940*. Cambridge: Cambridge University Press, 2005. EPUB edition.

Franzen, Jonathan. "What's Wrong With the Modern World." *The Guardian*,
13 September 2013. https://web.archive.org/web/20130915070641/
http://www.theguardian.com/books/2013/sep/13/jonathan-franzen-
wrong-modern-world.

Cook, Gareth. "Steven Pinker's Sense of Style." *Scientific American*, 30
September 2014. http://www.scientificamerican.com/article/steven-
pinker-s-sense-of-style/.

Harris, Michael. *The End of Absence: Reclaiming What We've Lost in a World of
Constant Connection*. s.l.: HarperCollins, 2014. EPUB edition.

Lacy, Sarah. "'Every Time Technology Changes, It Changes What People
in the Plot Can Do.' An Interview With Margaret Atwood." *Pando*, 30
August 2012. https://pando.com/2012/08/30/every-time-technology-
changes-it-changes-what-people-in-the-plot-can-do-an-interview-with-
margaret-atwood/.

Le Guin, Ursula K. "Staying Awake: Notes on the Alleged Decline of
Reading." *Harper's Magazine*, February 2008. http://harpers.org/
archive/2008/02/staying-awake/.

Lerner, Susan. "A Conversation with Jonathan Franzen." *Booth: A Journal*, 3 February 2015. http://booth.butler.edu/2015/02/13/a-conversation-with-jonathan-franzen/.

Levitin, Daniel J. *The Organized Mind: Thinking Straight in the Age of Information Overload*. New York: Dutton, 2014.

Oates, Joyce Carol. *You Must Remember This*. New York: Dutton, 1987.

Pinker, Steven. *The Sense of Style: The Thinking Person's Guide to Writing in the 21st Century*. New York: Viking, 2014.

Plato, *Phaedrus*, trans. Benjamin Jowett. s.l: n.p: 1997. EPUB edition.

Salmon, Felix. "To All the Young Journalists Asking for Advice." *Fusion*, 9 February 2015. http://fusion.net/story/45832/to-all-the-young-journalists-asking-for-advice/.

Self, Will. "The Novel is Dead (This Time It's for Real)." *The Guardian*, 2 May 2014. http://www.theguardian.com/books/2014/may/02/will-self-novel-dead-literary-fiction.

Solnit, Rebecca. *The Faraway Nearby*. s.l.: Penguin Group US, 2013. EPUB edition.

White, E.B. *Writings from The New Yorker 1927–1976*. New York: HarperCollins, 1990.

Zickuhr, Kathryn and Lee Rainie, "Younger Americans and Public Libraries." *Pew Research Center*, 10 September 2014. http://www.pewinternet.org/files/2014/09/PI_YoungerAmericansandLibraries_091014.pdf.

From Mush...
New Orleans
A Mixed Blood Highway
JOSEPH BOYDEN
ISBN 978-1-897126-29-5

The Old Lost Land
of Newfoundland
Family, Memory, Fiction, and Myth
WAYNE JOHNSTON
ISBN 978-1-897126-35-6

Un art de vivre
par temps de
catastrophe
DANY LAFERRIÈRE
ISBN 978-0-88864-553-1

The Sasquatch at Home
Traditional Protocols &
Modern Storytelling
EDEN ROBINSON
ISBN 978-0-88864-559-3

Imagining Ancient Women
ANNABEL LYON
ISBN 978-0-88864-629-3

Dear Sir, I Intend to
Burn Your Book
An Anatomy of a Book Burning
LAWRENCE HILL
ISBN 978-0-88864-679-8

Imagin...
TOMSON h...
ISBN 978-1-7721...

Who Needs Books?
Reading in the Digital Age
LYNN COADY
ISBN 978-1-77212-124-7

The Burgess Shale
The Canadian Writing
Landscape of the 60s
MARGARET ATWOOD
coming 2017

DATE DUE